The Big Hippo Guide to
Democracy, Referendums, General Elections
(and all that)

Bob Marshall Andrews and Martin Rowson

Published in the UK by Everything with Words Limited
3rd Floor, Descartes House, 8 Gate Street, London WC2A 3HP

www.everythingwithwords.com

Text copyright © Bob Marshall Andrews 2019
Illustrations © Martin Rowson 2019

Bob Marshall Andrews has asserted his right under the Copyright, Design and Patents Act 1988 to be identified as the author of this work.

This books is sold subject to the condition that it shall not, by way of trade or otherwise, be lent, resold, hired out, or otherwise circulated without the publisher's prior consent in any form of binding or cover other than that in which it is published and without a similar condition, including this condition, being imposed on the subsequent purchaser.

Printed and bound by Pulsio

A CIP catalogue record for this book is available from the British Library.

ISBN 978-1-911427-12-4

This is a story with no heroes, but here are some of the people you'll meet. None of them have got any magic, but some of them think they are **wizards**...

GENERAL ELECTIONS

This book is about **General Elections** and **Referendums**. It will help you to understand them. Hopefully...Perhaps.

General Elections are very important. If we did not have them, we wouldn't have a Government. If we did not have a Government we would be in an **Even Bigger Mess** than we are in now.

Possibly. Or it could be **CHAOS**. See **Big Hippo Guide to CHAOS THEORY**.

CALLING A GENERAL ELECTION

This is Roger. Roger is the **Prime Minister** which is very important as he is the leader of the majority of MPs in the House of Commons. One of the things Roger has to do is to decide when to call the **Next Election**.

Roger will do this when he thinks that he has the very best chance of winning the **Election**.

This is called **Acting in the National Interest**.

Roger

CAN ROGER CALL AN ELECTION?

Some people think that the Next Election cannot be called for **Five Years**, unless two thirds of Members of Parliament vote for it. Roger isn't supported by that number of MPs and therefore, some people think Roger cannot choose when to call an election.

This is what is called **A Common Political Misconception**.

Ever since Roger became Prime Minister, MPs opposing him have been saying that he is a rotten Prime Minister, that he is destroying the country and making most people poorer. They have been saying that Roger is a complete fool who could not run a stall selling Candy Floss. They say that he should resign and let them run things properly.

Here are some **Opposition MPs**.

Roger knows that if he calls for an early election those Opposition MPs will have to vote for it. Otherwise they will look very stupid. It is always important in politics not to look stupid. To look **VERY** stupid is even worse. **Much Worse**.

The Opposition

OPINION POLLS

These are carried out by **Opinion Pollsters**. They make a lot of money asking people for their opinions like 'How will you vote if there is an election tomorrow?' Then they take all the answers, add them up and announce the result to whoever has paid them to ask the questions.

It should be quite simple but it isn't. That is because the results are **WEIGHTED** depending on who the pollsters think are more likely to vote.

For instance, if you are **YOUNG** (18–25) it is thought that you are less likely to vote. This is because you are busy taking exams or drugs, getting drunk, going to parties or pop concerts or recovering from all of the above.

But if you are **OLD** (65–101) you are considered more likely to vote because you have nothing better to do than a spot of gardening, attempting to do a Sudoku, sleeping in a day centre or ringing Tesco Direct.

Here are pictures of **Young** and **Old Voters**.

Can you tell which is which?

Some of the Electorate—can you find them?

SOCIO ECONOMIC CATEGORIES

Also, people are divided by Opinion Polls into something called **SOCIO ECONOMIC CATEGORIES (A, B, Ci, and Cii)**. If you are an A, you are thought to be more likely to vote as you will be driven to the polling centre on the way to golf or shooting birds. If you are Cii, you are thought to be less likely to vote as you will be watching daytime television or in the betting shop or going next door to see your friend Tracy.

It is all highly scientific and based on many years of research and experience which is why pollsters can charge so much money and are relied on by Roger in deciding to call an election. **All in the National Interest**.

But sometimes, as I mentioned, everything goes wrong and the unpredictable just takes over as if it was the most natural thing in the world. Which perhaps it is, but for **CHAOS THEORY** and the **BUTTERFLY EFFECT**, see the **BIG HIPPO GUIDE TO CHAOS THEORY** which explains everything you didn't ever, ever want to know. Patiently. With lovely drawings.

Here is a picture of people in **Socio Economic Categories A and Cii**. Can you tell which is which?

STATESMANSHIP

All the opinion Pollsters (except one) tell Roger that he is miles in the lead and, if he calls an election, will win with a huge majority. Roger believes the polls for two reasons. First he thinks he is a very good Prime Minister (possibly the best ever). Second he thinks that the gentleman who leads the Opposition is a total **MUGWUMP**. This is a posh word for **INCOMPETENT IDIOT**.

Roger is almost certain that he will call an election, but before he does so, he does something very important. He announces that he will definitely **NOT** call an election. This is very clever. First, it makes **MUGWUMP** demand that Roger does call an election which means he must vote in favour of an election when Roger announces it.

Second, if Roger decides **NOT** to call an election, he will look **FIRM** and **CONSISTENT** which is very important in politics.

Simple isn't it?

Here is a picture of the **Leader of the Opposition**

MUGWUMP

SOLIDARITY AND COLLECTIVE RESPONSIBILITY

Here are Roger's Colleagues. They are all very important and are in charge of Government Departments like **Health** and **Home Affairs**. They are all given their jobs by Roger who can also sack them if, and when, he decides to do so.

For this reason, Roger hopes that they will agree with him. He calls this **Cabinet Government**. But of course, he might be in for a surprise!

Before he calls an Election, Roger **Consults his Colleagues**. In public, most of Roger's colleagues say most of the time that Roger is a very good Prime Minister and should be in charge at this time of national difficulty/peril/crisis caused by foreign countries and/or the opposition. In fact, almost all of them think he is an awful Prime Minister and lucky to have the job. For the time being.

But they all think that however dreadful Roger is, **MUGWUMP** is far, far worse. In their view most people would rather hurl themselves and their families from a cliff than elect **MUGWUMP** as Prime Minister. So they agree that he should call an election. This is called **Solidarity** or **Collective Responsibility**.

Roger is lucky. He has avoided **CHAOS** which might, of course, be lurking round the corner. A day is a long time in politics. Roger knows that sometimes an hour is even longer. It's amazing what can happen in an hour...

Cabinet or CHAOS

THE PRESS

One final thing that needs to be decided is **the Date of the Election**. This is important because it will set the length of the **Campaign** during which the political parties can persuade people to vote for them. Generally, this is between three and six weeks. Roger decides on six weeks. This is because he believes that the longer the campaign, the more people will realise that he is a very good Prime Minister and that **MUGWUMP** is utterly hopeless. This is called **A FINELY BALANCED DECISION**.

These are the **LADIES AND GENTLEMEN OF THE PRESS, EDITORS OF NATIONAL NEWSPAPERS**. They are considered to be very powerful and influential, at least by themselves. Most of them work for the owners of the newspapers who are called **PROPRIETORS**. Proprietors tend to be very rich people, who mainly come from somewhere else or live in strange places like the Channel Islands. Proprietors have very strong views on the **ELECTION**.

The editors share those strong views and so does everyone who works on the newspapers. That is lucky for them because otherwise they would be sacked.

This is called the **FREEDOM OF THE PRESS**. It's very important because otherwise we wouldn't be a democracy, would we?

The Press

OPINION FORMING

Because of their views, newspapers are often referred to as **leaning** one way or the other. Some of them lean so far they are in danger of falling over completely on their bottoms. (Many people believe that is the best place for them). When Roger calls the election, he knows that a number of newspapers will lean towards him and will help him to win the election. They do this by putting Strong Headlines in big letters at the top of their newspaper like **'MUGWUMP IN ISLINGTON GROOMING ENQUIRY'**. It doesn't matter what Mugwump has actually done as most people don't buy the newspaper but read the headline on a newsstand. This is called **Opinion Forming**. There are lots of ways of influencing how people think.

Here are people doing **Social Media**. You can see that those who are young can use two thumbs. Generally old people do not do social media. They think it is all about selling drugs, organising raves, cyber bullying and 'going viral' which sounds very dangerous if you are old.

Also they cannot use their thumbs like that which you have to learn before you are ten.

One of the things about social media is that you can put on it anything that you like and a lot of people will believe it.

For instance, in a General Election you can say **Mugwump to receive Mother Theresa Award for Compassion and Education**.

This is called **Fake News**.

Social Media

BERYL FROM BIRMINGHAM

Some people do **NOT** like **General Elections**. They think there are far too many of them and that they are a waste of time, money and energy. They think Roger should just get on with running the country.

Beryl from Birmingham is one of them.

Here is Beryl responding to the news that Roger has called another election.

It's lucky that Roger wasn't in Birmingham at the time isn't it?

Beryl from Birmingham

CANVASSING

When an **ELECTION** has been called people who are very keen supporters of the political parties go around knocking on other people's doors to find out how they are going to vote.

This is called **CANVASSING**.

This is Edwin. He is a keen supporter of Roger's party. He usually has a clipboard, a pencil and sheets of paper to help him canvass. On the paper he writes down whether people he has canvassed are **'For Roger'**, **'Against Roger'** or are **'Undecided'**.

This will help Roger to know whether he is winning the election or whether he has made a colossal **HORLICKS** calling the election at all.

Horlicks is an old fashioned word for **AN UNMITIGATED DISASTER**.

Edwin

EDWIN

This is Edwin actually canvassing.

The woman standing at the door is telling Edwin to **Go and get Lost**, before she lets the dog out to bite him.

Edwin will write down that the voter is **Undecided** whether to vote for Roger or not.

This called **Hopeless Political Optimism**.

Has Edwin called at your house?

Undecided

THE BBC

The BBC is very important in **General Elections** as it provides **Unbiased Political Commentary**. That means it must give fair time to all views, however silly. This is called **Public Sector Broadcasting**.

That does not stop some newspaper editors saying the BBC is totally biased. Perhaps they have forgotten the last headline in their newspaper. **'MUGWUMP IN TERROR PLOT AGAINST QUEEN'** which some people think is quite biased.

The BBC has programmes called things like **Today**, **World at One**, and **PM** at Five PM. This helps old people and people without watches to know what time it is. This is called **Public Information Broadcasting**.

Here are some **BBC Political Commentators**. The BBC is a **Public Corporation**. This means that these commentators are paid for by people like you and me.

BBC Commentators are paid a lot of money. Also the two on the left are paid lots more than the two on the right.

Can you see the difference between them? What is it?

The BBC

MANIFESTOS

Manifestos are very important in **General Elections**. They tell people what political parties will do if they win the election.

It is generally thought to be a good idea not to put too many details in your **Manifesto**. This is for two reasons:

First, you will be asked questions about the details. This means you have to remember the details to answer the questions which is not always easy.

Second, you might win the election. Then you may have to do what it says in the manifesto. This can be even more difficult.

Here is Roger answering questions on the details in his manifesto.

Roger has six weeks to answer questions about his manifesto. Roger may discover that a week is a long time in politics. Six weeks is a lot longer.

AND NOW FOR THE BIG EVENT!

All General Elections end on **Polling Day**.

Everyone in the country over eighteen years can vote, unless they are insane or a Lord, or both. They do this by going into a booth with a pencil and putting a cross against the candidate they want to be their MP.

It is a very worrying day for Roger because, whatever people have been told by the **Opinion Polls** or the **Newspapers** or the **BBC** or **Social Media** or **Canvassers** or **Manifestos**, they will, at the end of it all, when all is said and done, when the chips are down and when the fat lady has sung, vote for exactly who they like.

And that is called **DEMOCRACY**.

In any General Election there are a number of **MINORITY PARTIES**.

Here are the **LEADERS OF THE MINORITY PARTIES** with their manifestos. Their manifestos are full of details of the really big and new and expensive things they will do when they are in government.

This is fine for **Minority Manifestos** for two reasons.

First, they will not be asked questions about the details in the **Manifestos**. This is because the persons asking the questions will not have read them before they ask the questions.

Second, there is not the remotest chance that **Minority Parties** will be elected to power unless, in certain rare circumstances, they are invited to be part of a **Coalition Government**. This is called **Political Suicide**.

Minority Parties

REFERENDUMS

If Roger does not call a general election, he can still hold a **REFERENDUM**. Parliament has to vote for a referendum but it almost always does so. This is because anyone who votes against it will be accused of denying **THE PEOPLE THEIR SAY**.

Referendums are a bit like General Elections except that you don't vote for a party. You vote on a **SIMPLE** and **IMPORTANT** question which everyone understands such as

'Do you think a change in the Climate of 2% would be beneficial to the United Kingdom?'

Generally, there is a political reason for a referendum, like destroying an irritating political party you don't like or part of your own party. This is not always obvious from the question.

Before the referendum, there is a **REFERENDUM CAMPAIGN**. In the campaign both sides make big promises or very serious projections.

For instance, one side says a 2% change in climate will make us like Monte Carlo and £200 billion better off to spend on health and yachts or anything else.

The other side says that a 2% change will cause another **Ice Age** and force us to live in igloos and eat penguins.

Of course, as this is a referendum, these promises and projections are not in a party manifesto so you can promise or predict just about anything you like. If you win, you can always say that the promises or projections were the responsibility of someone else.

Alternatively, you can say that it is much, much more complicated than anyone thought. You can say, 'It is more complicated than the Schleswig Holstein Question'. Whatever that is.

Campaign Posters—all you need to know

THE RESULT OF THE REFERENDUM

As it is a straightforward vote on a **SIMPLE** and **IMPORTANT** question, the result should put an end to it. But this does not always happen...

For instance, if 50.01% vote for climate change and 49.99% vote against, then it might not put an end to it at all. This is particularly so if the promises and projections made in the campaign turn out to be **MASSIVE FIBS**.

This causes one side to say they have the **WILL OF THE PEOPLE** and the other to say it is the **DICTATORSHIP OF THE MAJORITY**.

In these circumstances things can get a little out of hand.

Perhaps the question ought to be:

'Do you think that Referendums are a good idea?'

What do you think?

The people have decided

A SERIOUS POLITICAL MUDDLE

Sometimes **General Elections** and **Referendums** can get a bit muddled up with each other. Sometimes this can be very serious.

This happens when Roger calls for an election to get a really big majority so that he can put the result of a referendum (as he sees it) into law. But if, in the end, he fails to get a majority **AT ALL** then there can be a **SERIOUS POLITICAL MUDDLE**.

This happens because all kinds of **Minority Parties**, who no-one had heard of, or cared about, suddenly become very powerful and insist on their own version of the referendum result before they vote for Roger's. Even worse, small groups of MPs in Roger's own party start to do the same. They often have funny names like **G-ERG** and look a bit odd.

Here are some **GERGs**.

Many people think this is very bad for Roger. It is certainly very bad for everyone else (except possibly some of the **GERGs**).

Many more people think it is a **NATIONAL DISASTER**.

Many people think that someone should **TAKE CONTROL**.

For someone to take control there should be a **General Election**.

(Which is what this little book is about.)

GERGs at large

Martin Rowson is a multi-award winning cartoonist and writer whose work has appeared regularly over the past 30 years in *The Guardian*, *The Times*, the *Daily Mirror*, *The Independent on Sunday*, *The Irish Times*, *Time Out*, *Tribune*, *The Spectator*, the *New Statesman*, *Morning Star*, the *Daily Express* and many other papers & periodicals. His books include graphic novelizations of *The Waste Land*, *Tristram Shandy*, *The Communist Manifesto* and *Gulliver's Travels*, while *Stuff*, his memoir about clearing out his late parents' house, was long-listed for the 2007 Samuel Johnson Prize for Non-Fiction.

Bob Marshall Andrews is a novelist, barrister and former Labour MP for Medway. His sharp comments have long made him known as the scourge of Westminster. Praise for *Off Message*, his account of his time as an MP:

'Full of wit, warmth, wisdom – and wine.'
– Ian Hislop

'Passionate, whimsical and highly entertaining'
– *The Observer*

'One of the most entertaining, irreverent, and magnificently self-indulgent political memoirs to emerge from the New Labour era'
– *The Times*

DO YOUR OWN REFERENDUM

Here's some space for you to jot down some good questions!

If you can't think of any, here are some suggestions.

- We should take back control from anyone else who pretends to be more important than us.
- Global warming is Fake News.

....

....

....

....

....

....

....

....

....

....

SPACE TO DO YOUR OWN FAKE NEWS!

This is to be done entirely on your own, without help from Trump, Putin, phoney liberals or anyone who claims to be an expert on anything. Anything at all. Time to just relax and use your imagination...

....
....
....
....
....
....
....
....
....
....
....
....
....